A Frugal Family:
500 Ways to Save Money

CW01502155

Keelan LaForge

storage and retrieval systems, without permission in writing from the publisher, except by reviewers, who may quote brief passages in a review.

Printed in Belfast, United Kingdom.
Publisher – Independently Published

As a single mum, I am always looking for inventive ways to save money, especially with the current Cost of Living crisis. Is it just me, or does everything feel unaffordable now? Sometimes I feel like being alive is too expensive! But I never get disheartened by it because I know that there is always room to improve on your budgeting and you can decide to turn it into a game rather than a chore. Sometimes, it's necessary to have a rewards system for yourself. If it works on kids, why wouldn't it work on adults too? It feels like I have come up with a million ways to save money in my time as a single parent, so I thought I may as well share a few of them. I love reading books about frugality and budgeting. Even if you've heard the ideas before, it helps to have them compiled in one place. Sometimes, I find that just reading frugal tips is enough to shift your mindset and help you get back on track. So, I thought I would challenge myself to list a five hundred ways to save money. I know that they must exist, and in compiling them, I hope it inspires you in your money-saving journey – and that it reminds me to stick to my budget too!

1.   Don't throw away potato or vegetable peelings. Use them to make vegetable stock, or coat them in oil, roast and salt them and eat them as crisps. My kids love these and throwing away peelings is something we often do without giving it a second thought, but why not turn them into a snack instead?

2.   Turn the radiators off in the Summer. Turn them down as low as you can in Winter. Use a hot water bottle when you're cold and ice packs from the freezer when you're hot. Run yourself a cool bath instead of having fans constantly running in your house. Stock up on the fluffiest blankets you can find and make your home as cosy as possible without the heating.

3.   Walk everywhere that you possibly can. Only use your car or public transport whenever it is a distance that is too far to walk. It will

save you so much petrol and it will save you the stress of finding a parking space too or waiting for a bus to turn up too!

4.   Turn off all the electronics in the house and do cheaper activities instead, like reading by candlelight, drawing, writing, playing a musical instrument, journalling, looking at recipe books, giving yourself a manicure, writing letters to friends. List as many cheap activities as you can and make time to do them.

5.   Use magazine clippings to make wall art. Keep postcards with pretty scenes on them and use them to decorate your walls. If you have imperfect surroundings, add cheap touches to make them look brighter and improve your mood.

6.   Don't host expensive events. You don't have to have an extravagant wedding, or an over-the-top birthday party. The thought behind it is what matters - not the expense.

7.   Don't buy expensive birthday cakes. Buy cake mix and make your own. Or buy a cheap cake and top it with sweets, icing and decorations to make it look special.

8.   Put all your money for bills into a separate account. Don't allow yourself to touch it unless you are withdrawing a payment for a bill date.

9.   Learn basic sewing and repair your clothes. Most clothing repairs are simple and going to a seamstress is incredibly expensive when you could easily do it yourself.

10.   Buy a body lotion that can be used for everything. Coconut oil can be used for both removing makeup and as a moisturiser

afterwards. It can also be used for cooking, but in that case, I wouldn't recommend using one pot for both! If you consolidate your products into versatile ones that cover many different bases, it is much less expensive than buying separate products for individual purposes.

11.   If you have kids, create a junk art box so they can be creative without costing you money on huge amounts of craft supplies. It's amazing how long a few empty boxes and some masking tape can entertain them for. My kids have never commented on a difference between a cheaper and more expensive craft project.

12.   Spend more time at home, or in your garden if you have one. Cut down on the amount of time you spend out and about, feeling tempted to spend money.

13.   Go out without a purse or wallet, or with a small amount of cash. If you leave your bank card at home, you can't come up with justification for using it on impulse buys.

14.   Switch to cheaper alternatives on the things you want to do. If you smoke, can you switch to rolling your own, or cut down on the number you have a day? If you're a coffee drinker, can you make your own half the time instead of going to the coffee shop every time? You don't have to entirely give up what you love; you can just cut the cost of it in ways that feel achievable.

15.   Bring picnics wherever you go. Any time you go out for the day, bring a supply of drinks, snacks and lunch. Make it easy for yourself to reach for whatever you already have instead of reaching for costly convenience foods. Pack cereal bars, dried fruit, crackers and things that you can keep in your bag all day without them going off. Pack chocolate or biscuits too so you don't pay for a sugary snack when you need one.

16.   Redefine what you consider to be fun. Make a challenge for yourself to stick to activities that are entirely free for one month and see how you feel by the end of it.

17.   Use what you already have. There have been so many times that I have gone out to buy something that I thought I needed, and I have later found it stashed in a cupboard somewhere. Check the cupboards first or be creative and think about how you can improvise and come up with your own solution.

18.   Have separate bank accounts for different things. Open an account in a different bank or buy bonds so you aren't always looking at the money you have as being "spendable." You might even forget it's there because you aren't seeing the figures each day and build up more interest or just get a pleasant surprise when you remember you have it.

19.   Make meals using whatever you have on hand instead of going to the shop for missing ingredients. Sometimes when you do this, they end up being surprisingly delicious. I recently made "chilli" with vegetarian mince, chickpeas and the spices I already had in the cupboard and it turned out really well.

20.   Explore your own area on foot. You'll probably be surprised by the number of places you come across or the things you've forgotten were just around the corner.

21.   Make full use of your library card. Don't let fines build up though. Use your library's app to read e-books and e-magazines online. You don't have to bring physical copies of books home if you don't want to – there are many options available online and audiobooks can be borrowed online too using the Libby app.

22.   Whenever you're washing your clothes, the suggested amounts of laundry powder are usually exaggerated to encourage consumers to use and buy more. If you use a tablespoon and use a couple of heaped spoonfuls of powder, it is more than enough to clean a load of laundry. You'd be surprised how fresh it smells when it comes out of the wash and a box of laundry powder will last an age if you use it like this. Apparently, overusing powder can clog your washing machine too, so there are other benefits to doing this.

23.   List every expense you've had in the last month and work out where you're wasting the most money. Put them in categories to make it easier to identify where your money is going.

24.   If you have a coffee maker and you use filter coffee, add a fresh scoop of coffee to half of the previous day's grounds if you're tight on money and still want fresh coffee. It doesn't make a noticeable difference to the taste.

25.   Buy own brand foods and products and see if you can really detect a difference. You might find that you prefer some of them to the name brand items you were using. I couldn't return to buying branded ketchup whenever the unbranded one is three pounds cheaper! Your tastebuds adapt to the taste of a different brand too.

26.   Rearrange your cupboards regularly so you can rotate the items hidden inside them and move items with closer expiry dates to the front.

27.   Make your kitchen an appealing replacement for a coffee shop. Buy whatever you need to feel like you can recreate the experience for yourself at home. If you go out for coffee, try to get in the habit of bringing your own cup because many coffee shops offer a discount when you use your own cup.

28.   Host dinner parties rather than eating out with friends and family. Make them easy for yourself if you don't like to cook or use them as a creative outlet if you do. Apart from the cost of ingredients and the use of the oven, cooking is a cheap hobby to cultivate. You need to eat anyway, so you might as well make it enjoyable.

29.   Make the most of what is in your local area. Redefine what counts as a day trip. You don't have to spend lots of money on petrol to get you to a pleasant destination. Use what you can around you.

30.   Make your own nature walks. You don't have to pay for expensive trails. You can find somewhere peaceful that's open to the public. If you have kids, give them natural items to find and turn it into a treasure hunt. Make it up as you go along and stop over-scheduling yourself and financially overstretching yourself.

31.   Our lives are so busy compared to fifty years ago. Even when I was a kid, we spent most of our time in the house or in the garden. If you attend to the things that need done around your home, you're less likely to go out as often and less likely to spend money. It means you procrastinate less too. Save days out for special days or just go for a simple walk when you feel the need to get out of the house.

32.   Go for cheap versions of luxuries. You don't need a twenty-foot paddling pool. Until recently, my kids still had a baby pool. They just sat on a chair with their feet in it in the summer. It wastes less water, and you can always go to a local pool when you get a chance. Any time I have got a larger paddling pool, my kids have lost interest in it by the time I've filled it, and it ends up getting torn and thrown out.

33.   Bring some sand and shells home with you when you got to the beach, and you can create a tiny beach play area in your garden. Add them to a water and sand table for extra interest. Alternatively, get your kids to paint the and use them to decorate your garden.

34.   Take cuttings from plants, use rooting powder and replant them. Plant edible things. Even having your own herbs on the kitchen windowsill can save you so much money on groceries.

35.   Turn flowering weeds from your garden into wild looking bouquets to brighten up your house.

36.   If you're going to throw something away, first, ask yourself if you could sell it or repurpose it into something else.

37.   Only do free exercise. You don't need a gym subscription (unless you want that to be one of your planned monthly luxuries, of course.) Go for long walks and runs in nature. Go for a bike ride on a cycle path. Do exercise videos at home and use your living room. It will still have the exact same effect on you, but you will have saved yourself a lot of money and effort (I always dread entering changing rooms at the gym, so it cuts out that part too.)

38.   Stop and notice the beauty around you. Get rid of items on your to-do list. Take time to notice the sounds and sights around you. By doing that, you can turn something simple into free entertainment. Find a quiet spot to sit in in the park, bring a drink and read in the sun, or just watch the sky and see how much activity is going on around you in nature.

39.   Find a boxset included in your subscription and take the time to watch it. Don't be tempted to spend extra money outside of that. Try to create a home cinema experience so you don't want to go to the real cinema. Create a weekly movie night in your house that you and your kids can look forward to.

40.   Make your own pizza. It's so easy – especially if you have a mixer with a dough hook. If you can't be bothered making dough and letting it rise, made a soda bread pizza base. If you don't have buttermilk, you can add a tablespoon of vinegar or lemon juice to

regular milk and leave it to sit for a few minutes to make it curdle. It works with non-dairy milk too.

41.   If you feel the urge to eat out, have a snack before you go and order a smaller portion or a dessert instead. Try to eat at off-peak times, like a weekday evening. Look for early bird menus or have lunch or breakfast instead. Look for hidden gems in your city or village. Watch out for expensive drinks and order cordial or water. Go to "bring your own bottle" places or wait until you get home to have drinks, coffees or chocolates.

42.   Set no spend challenges for yourself. Sometimes a whole month or year can be too daunting to feel achievable. Aim for a no-spend day or week instead. Reward yourself with inexpensive treats at the end of it.

43.   Schedule payments to automatically go into your savings account so you don't have to think about transferring them.

44.   Spend your time doing things that feed your spirit rather than draining your bank account. Journal, scrapbook, paint, walk beside the sea, make up recipes of your own.

45.   Get toiletries in the pound shop. Their body lotion is surprisingly good, and they have a good range of products that cost much more elsewhere. You can create a home spa, so you don't feel tempted to pay to visit a real one.

46.   Invest in things you will use repeatedly. For example, I bought a sewing machine, which to me is a big purchase, but the amount of money it has saved me in being able to fix my own clothes and to make alterations to things and in making my own curtains has been huge.

47.   Be open to accepting second hand items. I've been lucky enough to get a bread maker, two coffee pots, a deep fryer and lots of

lovely clothes that my mum wasn't using. Sometimes the things that you get for free end up being the things you love the most. I think there is a false belief that you need to spend a lot for something to be worthwhile, but sometimes the best things in life really are free.

48.   Be careful with money traps. Sometimes offers are displayed in shops that make things appear cheap whenever they are in fact, much more expensive than items that aren't on offer.

49.   Be selective about what you agree to do. Prioritise the people that mean most to you and practise saying no to the things that you can't afford to do, financially or emotionally.

50.   Don't feel pressured by the amounts of money you see people around you spending. You don't know how much debt they have, and overspending can often be a way to overcompensate for other more important areas that are lacking in someone's life. Focus on the simple things you have that mean a lot to you and disregard what other people are doing. Their lives probably aren't as perfect as they appear to be from the outside, or even if they are, you are living your own life anyway. There's no point in trying to emulate someone else's. Make your own life pleasant instead.

51.   Make drinks you want to drink at home. Sometimes I think that people fall into the habit of getting takeaway drinks all the time because they are more appealing than what they have in the house. Not spending any money on drinks for your house can be a false economy when you end up spending more on single use drinks in cafes and shops instead.

52.   Consider how much hot water you are using. I used to have a habit of showering multiple times a day, but it isn't necessary. I still shower each day and wash again if I want to feel fresher, but it has halved my electricity bill, just by cutting down on constant showering, and my skin feels softer too because I'm not stripping it of all its natural oils.

53.   Have cooler baths in the summer. Only use the amount of hot water you need.

54.   If you do have membership of a swimming pool or gym, wash and dry your hair there to save money on energy at home.

55.   Go to coffee mornings in local churches. There are many community hubs that have been set up since the pandemic to provide coffee, tea, conversation and warmth for people. Look around your local area for community projects like that.

56.   Do simple DIY projects by yourself. Even if you aren't that way inclined, there are easy upcycling projects you can do at home. Pick up books on it from the library. They always seem to have an expansive collection of books on simple DIY. The best way to learn is to try and see what works and what doesn't.

57.   Look out for things that people are throwing away. I bumped into a lady I know recently that was carrying a piece of furniture she had found in a skip. It was about to go to landfill, but it was a sturdy piece of shelving that just needed some sanding and painting to look brand new.

58.   Save seeds from fruits you eat and plant your own trees and bushes. Keep them inside until they are strong enough to survive outside. (I shouldn't be giving advice on how to keep plants alive, but I have learnt a few mistakes through doing them myself!)

59.   Have swaps with friends. If you are giving things away, consult each other first and let each other have first pick. Sometimes you will find your favourite items in someone else's donation bag and vice versa.

60.   Consider charity shopping for presents. Sometimes you find the most thoughtful presents second hand and you can find items that

you couldn't afford to buy new that haven't been used once and that are still sealed and in their original packaging.

61.   Go charity shopping in affluent areas. You will find so many discarded treasures there and often I find that they are under-priced, so you can pick up unnoticed bargains.

62.   Read as much as you can. It costs nothing, other than the cost of the books, and if they're from the library, they're free.

63.   Look at all your subscriptions regularly. Check your bank account for recurring payments. Do you still use them? Could you delete any of them?

64.   Withdraw the amount of cash you want to spend for the week. Only use that, and when it's done, don't withdraw any more or fall back into the habit of using your card again.

65.   Don't pay for extra services that you don't need. If any of your bills go up, call the company and discuss switching to a cheaper option.

66.   Don't use lights unnecessarily. Open the blinds and let every ounce of sunlight in that you can. Sit outside on warm evenings. Use candles or rotate your lamps. Don't use them all at once. Make a habit of turning lights off every time you leave a room. Get battery operated lights and fairy lights to cut down on your use of electricity.

67.   Make listening to music an activity. Spend days searching for new music you like. Make playlists for different moods. It's a cheap way to pass time and you will uncover so many wonderful pieces of music you might never have found otherwise.

68.   Switch everything off at the wall when you aren't using it or whenever you go out or go away for the night. Don't let energy get used up for no good reason.

69.   Write letters to the people you care about. They will be touched by them and it's a satisfying way to connect with someone without spending a lot of money.

70.   Give people your time rather than your money. Go for a walk with a friend, bring home-baked treats to their house, offer to babysit for someone, invite them over to your garden for some wine or tea. People value the time you give them more than the gifts you buy. Most gifts end up being forgotten anyway. Unless someone has the rare ability to buy gifts that fit your personal taste, many gifts end up being set aside and not used or donated to charity. Give resources to people that you know they really need.

71.   Don't buy individually packed snacks. Cheese tastes the same whether it comes in one large block or whether it's in individually portioned plastic. Don't spend an extra few pounds just to save yourself the time it takes to cut a slice of cheese. You'll be helping the environment too.

72.   Come up with lists of as many activities as you can think of that you love to do and that don't cost a penny. Think of your favourite times and remind yourself of ideas you might have forgotten about.

73.   Get a day ticket for the bus and take it wherever you like. Explore parts of your city you don't know. Find new parks, bookshops, libraries and amenities. We can easily get into the habit of always going to the same places and doing the same things. Sometimes, you just need to liven things up by thinking outside the box.

74.   Enter as many competitions as you can. If you do them regularly, it's likely that you will win one. We have won a box of donuts before, a shopping centre voucher and a couple of Christmas hampers. It mightn't always work out, but it's another activity to do on a day when you might have been spending money instead.

75.   Volunteer your time to help others. It doesn't have to be a huge commitment. You could help with gardening in your kid's school, write book reviews for the library, help a neighbour with errands or make art for your friends.

76.   When you go shopping, look for ideas rather than impulse buys. Make a list of the things you would like to get and revisit it a week later to see if it is still a real desire of yours.

77.   Make iced tea and cordial with ice cubes at home. They feel like fancy, refreshing drinks, but they are both much cheaper than fizzy drinks and other soft drinks.

78.   Think before you pay. Stop yourself before each purchase and ask yourself if it is essential or if you could find it cheaper elsewhere, or entirely do without it.

79.   Have regular clear-outs. As well as bringing you mental clarity and physical space, you will be reminded of the things you own that lurk at the back of cupboards. Many of these items can be sold or used when you'd forgotten you even had them.

80.   Keep track of your spending. Keep a note of each expense in your phone so you don't forget anything. Read through it and be honest with yourself about how it makes you feel.

81.   Find cheaper alternatives to the things you would like to do but that feel too expensive. Book a trip near home if you want to go abroad but you know the cost of it will cause you stress. Go for a day trip rather than paying for a hotel. Look for free events to attend in your area.

82.   Don't take up hobbies you can't afford. Start with projects you already have the materials for.

83.   Search for discount codes every time you make an online purchase. Google items you're buying to make sure there isn't a cheaper one elsewhere that you have missed.

84.   Only buy things that you truly need or truly love.

85.   Make your own ice lollies at home. Use fizzy drinks that have gone flat rather than throwing them out. Use cordial and freeze it. Freeze yogurts with lolly sticks pushed through the lids. Your kids will love them, and it will save you constantly buying them.

86.   Never throw away fruit that is beginning to turn. Freeze it and use in smoothies and desserts. Peel bananas first and freeze them to make smoothies and banana ice-cream. Use oranges for freshly squeezed orange juice.

87.   Instant coffee has got so expensive recently. Consider getting own brand fresh coffee instead and get yourself a cafetiere or a coffee pot. You don't need a fancy espresso machine to have good coffee (but if that stops you getting a takeaway coffee a day, it's still worth doing.)

88.   Go for picnics and barbecues in good weather instead of eating out. Bring all the supplies you need so you don't end up having to buy anything while you're out. Get a disposable barbecue to make it easier for yourself.

89.   Make a list of low-cost activities in your area and display it on the wall, to remind yourself of them whenever you're at a loss for what to do. Sometimes it is hard to think of them in the moment, especially with kids screeching in your ear! Have it right in front of you so you can quickly pick somewhere to go that doesn't charge entry fees.

90.   Keep your petrol tank half full instead of filling it fully. It makes the car more efficient, and it keeps the car lighter, so it uses less

petrol. Empty the boot of your car too. Don't carry around extra weight you don't need.

91.   Make your home as uncluttered as possible. Make it somewhere you want to be, so you aren't tempted to go out all the time. If you have an outdoor space, make a seating area, however small, so you have somewhere to sit in the sun. Change things around so you don't get bored of looking at the same stuff all the time.

92.   Hang your clothes to dry as often as you can. Minimise using a dryer unless it's essential.

93.   Only iron items you can't get away with not ironing! It is using electricity too, and if it isn't noticeably creased, there's no need to waste the time and energy on it.

94.   Buy the cheapest bread you can find for toast. Unless you want some kind of deli loaf, bread mostly tastes the same toasted. Plastic bread is plastic bread.

95.   Check sites like Wowcher. It's a little more effort, but you can find discounted tickets to local attractions, offers on meals and gifts for much less than you will get them from the company. Just remember to complete the redemption process!

96.   Buy candle dupes. Candles can get so expensive, and there are some very heavily scented copies out there. I usually find that the expensive candles tend to smoke a lot too. I find a lot of £3 candles with long burning times and strong scents. Lighting one makes your house feel much more homely.

97.   Improvise with what you have at home. If your kid needs a costume for school, see what you have on hand. With a bit of creativity, it's amazing what you can come up with. My daughter had a Greek day in school, so I just found a Greek-looking dress in a charity shop, added some jewellery and a hairband! It was cheap but she

looked great and loved her costume. Had we bought a ready-made one online, it would have cost much more, and it was only for one day. There's no point in overspending on something you will only use once.

98.   Redefine what you consider to be a party. Have smaller parties at home for your kids. Let them choose a close friend to bring and make them feel special and treasured instead of putting all your energy and resources into entertaining a crowd of party guests. Some of my kids' favourite birthdays have been very simple and cheap: a friend, a couple of party games, some cocktail sausages and a cake. Or take them on a little day trip and give them a budgeted amount of money to spend on whatever they like. Kids just want to feel like the star of the show on their birthday, and that isn't a feeling you can create with your bank card.

99.   Make your own greetings cards. Buy supplies from the pound shop and make personalised cards for friends and family. It will mean much more, gives you a hobby to work on and you can use the card-making supplies over the course of the year. Be careful in shops that don't have clear price tags on things. Don't let the shop assistant make you feel pressured into buying things that are over your budget. Alternatively, buy cards from budget card shops that sell ten cards for a pound. Think ahead and get cards that suit different people with upcoming birthdays. Reuse gift bags too.

100.   Just because you have a look in a shop, it doesn't mean you are obligated to buy something. Try to become comfortable with having a look around, saying a friendly thank you and walking away.

101.   Don't buy recipe books. You can google every recipe you'll ever need and there are so many videos on YouTube that guide you through recipes. Unless you have a favourite one, recipe books usually just take up shelf space and collect dust. If you want to get one, try getting it from the library first, see if you actually make any of the recipes from it and only buy it if you know you will regularly use it.

102.   Keep a notebook of your favourite recipes and keep it in your kitchen drawer. It is a helpful reminder of what you like to make, and you can easily reach for it whenever you're at a loss for what to cook.

103.   Adopt the attitude that people had towards clothing and possessions a century ago. Invest in one quality item over twenty cheap items. You don't need duplicates of everything. Get one good swimsuit you love, one pair of walking boots, one teapot. We tend to collect things as if we are saving up for a natural disaster or something, but if you are honest with yourself, how many of the items do you regularly use?

104.   Join rewards programmes like the Amazon Shopper Panel. If you sign up for it, you can receive vouchers for answering simple survey questions.

105.   Never leave old devices lying unused in a drawer. Always trade them in and get money off your next contract or extra cash you can use towards your next phone.

106.   Use things until they are completely done or finished. Don't throw away almost empty bottles of toiletries or almost empty jars of peanut butter. Don't get rid of clothes that can still be worn or items that don't need to be replaced.

107.   Don't let the weather hold you back. Go for walks in blustery weather. Bring a picnic in the car or find shelter under the boughs of a tree. Don't let the weather drive you indoors to pay for expensive activities all the time.

108.   Think of new ideas for dates instead of going for expensive meals and trips. Watch the sunset, walk along the shore, bring a picnic with you, have drinks together in the garden, lie under the stars, visit the museum, lie on the grass together.

109.   Retrain your mind to get excited about the simplest things in life. You don't have to spend a lot of money to have a rich life. Read magazines and books that foster that mindset. Get The Simple Things magazine and take inspiration from it on how to fill your day with enriching experiences that cost very little. Watch YouTubers that make videos about frugality to help encourage that mindset.

110.   Don't pay for the quickest fix. Have a look at your options first. Don't jump into anything and take your time to pick the most cost-effective option.

111.   Don't have a credit card. Don't get store cards. Try to live on the money you have and save for the things you don't.

112.   If you're eating out, scan the menu for the cheapest options. Don't read the rest.

113.   Make use of savers menus in fast food places. Bring your own water with you. If you are paying to eat in, no one is going to challenge you for having a drink of water. If they do, just ask for tap water.

114.   Cut out processed snacks. You'll be amazed by how much money you save just by doing this.

115.   Stop buying bottled water and juice. Make up your own bottle at home.

116.   Make a habit of taking your own flask of tea or coffee to the park instead of going to coffee shops and getting takeaway coffees.

117.   Pick a money-draining habit to stop for a month and see how much difference it makes to your finances.

118.   Stay with friends and family whenever you can. When you travel, try to visit people you know when you take a trip. You'll get a holiday and a catch up at the same time.

119.   Stop buying more food than you need. How many items of food do you throw out a week? How many unused packets of food are lying stagnating in your cupboards? Cook from your pantry and freezer for as long as you can and set yourself a no groceries challenge.

120.   Learn how to patch holes, how to darn and how to sew seams. They are all much easier to do than you would think, and it means if something tears, you don't have to throw it away.

121.   Don't buy your kids toys unless it is their birthday, Christmas or a special celebration.

122.   If you want to give your kids a treat, give them a pounds to spend in the pound shop. They will love the challenge of trying to find the best thing they possibly can for their tight budget. Do the same for yourself.

123.   Sell as many items in your house as you can. If they aren't being used, list them online. There are so many places to do this nowadays. Don't leave items unloved and unutilised. You'd be surprised by how many items in your house are sellable and wanted by other people.

124.   Write all your uncomfortable feelings onto paper. Don't direct them into budget breaking habits like impulse buying, drinking or partying.

125.   Appreciate everything you already have around you. Take time to note down everything you appreciate in your life. It is an activity that keeps you busy, and you will make you less inclined to pointlessly spend money.

126.   Instead of going out for brunch, learn how to make the things you love at home. Learn how to make great pancakes, invest in a waffle iron, make French toast, buy fancier bread if it makes it more

appealing. You will still save a fortune compared with dining out. If you think about it, most cafes charge about ten pounds for a plate of French toast. It is just bread with egg on it and syrup.

127.   Learn how to make iced coffee. Make an iced coffee mix so you can whip it up quickly at home. You just need to mix instant coffee with sweetener and boiled water, let it cool and keep it in the fridge. Then, all that's left to do is add milk and ice.

128.   Don't go overboard with presents for your children. Get them one main present and a few token things. They will enjoy their presents much more because they won't be overwhelmed by them. They will also be less likely to break their toys because they will value them more.

129.   Limit screentime. Try to do fun things with your kids that don't involve charging, downloading or streaming.

130.   Get used to shopping just to have a look and get ideas. Make lists and take photos of items you like. Wait to buy them and see if the photo is enough to satisfy you.

131.   Don't be proud or precious about what you bring into your home. Just because you found something that was discarded by someone, it doesn't make it rubbish, nor should you feel small for taking help from friends and family that wish to offer it.

132.   List any clothes you aren't using on Vinted. Even if they only sell for a couple of pounds, it all adds up if you keep consistently doing it. Put any earnings from it straight into a savings account and start to build up an emergency fund if you don't already have one.

133.   Check Facebook Marketplace and Gumtree before making new purchases. You might find one that is just as good and lightly used for a fraction of the price.

134.   Use clothes horses whenever you can. Don't use energy you don't need to use. Spend a little more time to save a little money. It doesn't have to be permanent – you can do it at the times you need to save a little extra cash.

135.   Set a challenge for yourself to live below your means. Put the remaining money into a savings account or a jar at the end of the week. You'll be surprised by how quickly it mounts up.

136.   Look for cheaper alternatives to fancy meals. You can experiment with new recipes and buy high quality ingredients for much less than you would spend on a meal in a restaurant. Get a takeaway with friends instead of meeting up in a restaurant. Think about the number of amazing meals you have eaten in restaurants in your life. How many times have they surpassed your expectations? Usually, I find that meals at home taste better and fresher. If you are going to eat out, go to a set price buffet. Then, you can eat as much as you like, and it will always cost the same.

137.   Make presents for people instead of automatically going to the shop. What are you good at? Is there a way in which you can turn it into a gift for someone else?

138.   Get a bird sounds app and spend time identifying the birds in your area. Make cheap toilet paper roll bird feeders with peanut butter and oats. Hang them up in your garden and enjoy watching the wildlife in your surroundings.

139.   Play garden games in the summer. Stock up on games like badminton, frisbee, chalk for drawing on the ground, swing ball or a sand tray. The more time you spend at home, the less time you spend out in the world spending money.

140.   Volunteer in your local church. Even if you aren't religious, you can still help out. They are always looking for volunteers to entertain the kids and to help host fairs, etc. It will give you a sense of purpose

and a project to work on and some new friends in your community. Not every fun day out has to cost you money. Spend time before you spend money and people will appreciate it more.

141.   Give gifts of time to your loved ones. Make jars filled with paper promises of things you will do to make their day better: offer babysitting services, offer to make dinner, have them over for coffee and treats, offer to do an errand they'd rather not do.

142.   Whenever I was in school, I had a friend that came up with a present called a Happiness Jar. We made them for each other and filled them with sweets, confetti, glitter and little trinkets to cheer each other up. They were incredibly cheap to make, and they are such thoughtful gifts. You're never too old to receive a jar of happiness!

143.   Turn your garden or porch into a mini bar and save whatever money you might have been tempted to spend in a beer garden. Make ice cubes, get a wine cooler or pick up some fancy glasses in charity shops to make your drinks feel a little bit more special.

144.   If you have oil heating, top up the tank whenever the prices dip or in the summertime. Buy what you need and a little more. You don't have to fill everything to the top all the time. If you apply this to any of your shopping, you will notice a big difference in your savings.

145.   If you have kids, sign them up for summer camps in churches before looking into expensive summer schemes. They will still get to play, make friends and burn off some energy, so it achieves the same thing, but at a fraction of the cost.

146.   Know when it's ok to spend money. Sometimes making a purchase can save you money in the long run. Investing in a quality appliance might seem costly at the time but spread out over the number of years it lasts for, it becomes much cheaper and more efficient.

147.   Don't pay for expensive classes. You can learn anything you want to learn online now. You can pick up any skill by watching YouTube and practising while you watch. There are also websites like Domestika that offer classes at affordable rates.

148.   Consider getting a pass to a local estate, farm or centre. If you compare most annual memberships to paying for an individual visit, the cost is miniscule compared with the cost of a single trip pass. For example, to visit the local open farm with my kids would cost about £25 for one visit. I bought us a summer pass which lasted from May until September and it was £90 for all of us (and we could go as often as we liked.)

149.   Don't assume that because something is second hand it isn't any good. I have spent a lot of money on new clothes that have torn after one wear, and I have found £3 treasures in charity shops that I've worn hundreds of times.

150.   Know when to save things you might need again and when to throw things away. I have a tendency to hold on to things I might need, but the clutter gets to me, and I spend less time at home whenever the place isn't clutter-free. Sometimes saving everything can be a false economy and you just lose everything in your house and get overwhelmed.

151.   Get creative with gift wrapping. Make your own stamped wrapping paper with the kids or use coloured tissue paper. Find cheaper alternatives that are still pretty and serve the same function.

152.   Save drinking alcohol for a weekly or monthly treat. Don't drink every night out of habit. It's a costly activity and you will savour it more if you make it something you do less often.

153.   Have a filling meal and plenty to drink before you go grocery shopping, so you don't make hunger buys.

154.   Allow your kids to suggest one item whenever they come with you to the shop but don't put everything in the trolley just because they told you to.

155.   Stick with a smaller house. Don't buy a bigger house than you need. Apart from the costliness of the buy, you'll spend much more on heating and maintenance. Keep it small and manageable for yourself.

156.   Attend to your mental health. There are so many ways to look after your mental wellbeing without spending money. Do guided meditation, yoga, pilates, draw a picture or write down your worries. Keeping your mind healthy means you'll be less likely to spend money to make yourself feel better.

157.   Do rock painting. It can be turned into a day-long activity with a trip to the beach, beachcombing, painting and varnishing if you want a shiny finish.

158.   Spend a little more time on things to save money. It takes longer to hang your washing out on the line and to iron it, but it's cheaper than running your dryer all the time.

159.   Only read books from second-hand book shops and the library. Save buying new books for a birthday treat. It's costly whenever they will probably end up looking second hand by the time you've finished with them anyway.

160.   Don't use your overdraft. Don't view it as extra money.

161.   Bring a water bottle with you wherever you go and bring water and snacks for your kids.

162.   Eat simpler foods. If you buy fruit, cereal and crackers, etc for snacks, you will waste much less money on food that is only to tide you over until mealtimes. Allow yourself to feel hungry sometimes; it makes eating a meal much more satisfying.

163. If you are asked what you'd like for your birthday, ask for vouchers for experiences. It means you can eat out or go to activities more affordably and you'll look forward to them if you reserve them for special occasions.

164. If you're tempted to order takeaway, try to create your own at home instead. Invest in items that make it easier to satisfy your takeaway craving. For example, we have a deep fryer and I use it to make chips and deep-fried chicken so we can create more convincing fakeaway options at home.

165. Sell any clothes or shoes you haven't worn in six months.

166. List items you're selling on more than one site. It increases your chances of making a sale – just remember to delete the item off all the sites once it has sold!

167. Check Olio for food and non-food items. Reserve in bulk to make your car journey worthwhile.

168. Consider getting a pet. You will be more likely to spend your time doing free activities, like walking your dog or taking it to a dog park or sitting in the house with your cat for company. Looking after pets can become a hobby for kids and it keeps them occupied and teaches early responsibility.

169. Shop around for carparks. Investigate to see which has the lowest prices. Some carparks have deals where they charge a set fee all day if you arrive before a certain time.

170. Make sure you're getting all the benefits you are entitled to. You might assume you aren't entitled to any, but if you phone Make the Call, you might find out there is a payment you qualify for.

171.   Take good care of your teeth so you don't have to spend unnecessarily on dental treatments.

172.   Dye your own hair, start practising cutting your hair, do your own home manicures and pedicures. Get whatever products you need to make this easier.

173.   Don't deprive yourself of treats all the time. Treat yourself to a donut from the shop or a bun from the bakery or a packet of sweets. It's much cheaper than waiting until you feel deprived and then splurging on an expensive meal or going on a shopping spree instead.

174.   If you feel the urge to shop, try and direct that energy into selling or donating items instead. Allow yourself to buy one item from a charity shop after browsing around and looking at all the available options. Make thoughtful purchases.

175.   If you're feeling bored, go for a brisk walk or make something using supplies you already have at home. Don't go shopping for entertainment.

176.   If you need to buy one thing, think about ways to substitute it with what you already have at home. Try to avoid entering a shop at all costs. Most outings for one item end in bags full of groceries. It's best to just avoid putting yourself in the situation in the first place.

177.   Make a list of all the free activities in your area. Make researching them an activity in itself.

178.   Make a list of all the things that make you happy that don't involve spending money. Sometimes you just need to take the time to remember them.

179.   Invite friends over or have meet-ups at the park and bring your own coffee and snacks, or go to the library or an art gallery together. Save paying for activities for whenever you really want to do

them – not just so you have somewhere to meet up. Your friend is the reason for your meet-up; not the location.

180.   Agree on a gift budget with friends and family. Make it into a challenge to see what you can get for your friend for five pounds or less.

181.   Rethink how you prepare lunches and dinners. Reduce the amount of meat you use. Cook a whole chicken and use small amounts each day, bulked out with pulses and vegetables.

182.   Take on small side jobs to earn some extra money. Offer to babysit, teach a subject you studied, sell art online or propagate plants and sell them.

183.   Have no car days. Save the car for a big day out like people used to do in the past. It will feel special if you do that and you won't have to constantly top up your petrol.

184.   Use warm colours in your home to make it look cosy and cheerful. Make it somewhere welcoming and pleasant to spend time.

185.   Light plenty of candles (so long as you're keeping an eye on them, and they aren't next to anything flammable!) It's a cheap way to create light and warmth around you.

186.   Don't jump to spend money when you're looking for things to do. Think outside the box and come up with as many cheap alternatives as you can. They will likely be much more memorable too. A homemade picnic in your garden with friends is much more memorable than one of many trips to a samey shopping centre or a generic restaurant.

187.   Start a magazine recycling circle with friends or family. You'll always have a new one to read but you will only have to buy one.

188.   Get together all your unwanted items and bring them to a car boot sale. It's usually cheap to get a space at one and your trash can become someone else's treasure.

189.   Make your own wall displays with dream boards and images you find inspiring. You can add to it as you come across more and more items you like. Looking at it each day will keep you focused on your goals and help you to financially achieve them.

190.   Have a balloon fight with your kids/with your friends on a hot day. You're never too old to act like a kid. Get in the paddling pool to cool down. It will lift your mood and on a hot day, it provides relief from the heat. You can get a cover for it, so you don't have to continuously empty and refill it.

191.   Ration treat items so they last longer and you're having them the way they were meant to be consumed. For example, having a couple of squares of chocolate with a cup of tea and taking the time to savour it feels no different to eating an entire bar in a hurry.

192.   Have a board game party. Pick up games from charity shops and car boot sales. You can often find unused ones that people have given away after Christmas, etc.

193.   Keep on top of things that need attended to. If you deal with them in their early stages, it's more likely you won't have to pay a huge amount later to fix a much bigger problem.

194.   Spend more time shopping around for cheaper options. Don't jump to buy the most expensive thing simply because it takes less time.

195.   Practise the art of adding desired items to your online basket without checking out.

196.   When you're about to go to the till in a shop, reassess what you've put in your basket or trolley. Try to put back as many items as you can. Ask yourself if you have an alternative at home or if you can entirely do without it.

197.   Before you throw something out, ask yourself if it is truly done? Is it better off in landfill than in your house? Use items until they are done – don't just replace them because it feels like it's time for a new one.

198.   Make a bucket list for the year of all the activities you want to do. Save for the costly ones that are most important to you and then work out how you can avoid spending any money the rest of the year to budget for them.

199.   Make use of natural spaces. Most of them are free to visit. Go to the beach, the forest and the mountains. Think ahead and bring the supplies you need for the day. Bring home pine cones, shells and pretty leaves as souvenirs and make seasonal displays in your house for free.

200.   Reward yourself for not spending money. Make yourself a treat at home whenever you have a no spend day, or whenever you manage to avoid spending money on something you would normally waste money on.

201.   Start a blog about your lifestyle. If you track your money journey, it will inspire you to keep going and connect you with others with the same frame of mind.

202.   See how many useful or fun items you can find in a charity shop for less than five pounds.

203.   Before you buy new, look in charity shops first. There are so many things I have found in charity shops that would have been much more expensive new, and I wouldn't necessarily have thought I could

find them second hand – I just stumbled upon them. For example, a music stand for my daughter, a coffee maker, school uniforms, etc.

204.   Join frugality groups on Facebook or elsewhere online. You'll be amazed by how many inventive tips people share. It helps you to change your mindset, start saving and get more creative.

205.   Spend time with people that uplift you, not with people that drain you. Whenever we feel drained, we are more likely to spend recklessly.

206.   Wash your own car and clean it inside. It will save you so much money when you're trying to pinch pennies. It's satisfying seeing the results of your efforts too.

207.   Over-budget for bills. Set the money aside in a separate account. You won't view it as spending money because you know it's just for bills, and the extra will quickly add up.

208.   Look for rewards programmes whenever you are taking out insurance through comparison sites. You can get apps that allow you to get large discounts on coffee, eating out and cinemas. For example, compare the market offer 25% discounts on Café Nero and discounts on Pizza Hut, etc.

209.   If you go anywhere regularly, get the app. You will almost always get a free item after buying a certain number of items from the place. (The Café Nero and Starbucks apps, Boots and Pizza Express, to name a few.)

210.   Learn a skill that produces items you can sell, like knitting, jewellery making or card making. Putting your time and energy into activities like that focuses you so you can't spend money out of boredom.

211.   If you are eating out or going out for coffee, go for the smaller cup or the smaller serving or the cheapest option on the menu.

212.   If you read a magazine often or if you use a service often, get a subscription so you can benefit from the discount.

213.   Spend time with people that have similar financial goals to yours. Don't surround yourself with people that lead expensive lifestyles or that are in huge amounts of debt.

214.   Think about what your true values are. Write them down and decide if you're living your life in line with them or if there are fundamental changes you could make.

215.   Read books and watch videos on frugality. Surround yourself with inspiring influences to motivate you to stay on track.

216.   Use a rental company for something expensive you only need as a one off. There's no point in wasting hundreds of pounds on something you will only use for one event. You can hire anything nowadays, from bikes to wedding dresses.

217.   Use smaller portions of meat or fish in your cooking. Use them to enhance the flavour rather than as the main component of a meal. You will be surprised by how much money you save.

218.   Only buy things for your house whenever you can picture exactly where they'll go when you get home.

219.   Always have staples in your cupboard. You can do a lot with some tinned tomatoes, some tuna and some rice or pasta.

220.   Make home remedies for sickness. I find lemon and ginger tea with some honey in it more effective for colds than any over the counter medication you can get.

221.   If you're getting tired of your clothing, make easy alterations to it. Add different buttons, sew on some patches, add some ribbon or trim. Save any fabric scraps so you have them whenever you want to do a simple project. Then, you won't have to venture into an expensive craft store too, only to find yourself returning home with half the shop.

222.   Find out about reading groups in your area or in the library, for yourself or for your kids. It's a great way to motivate you to read more and to get involved in discussing books with others. It's a cheap way to pass time and you'll probably get some tea or coffee and a biscuit too!

223.   Look out for items people are giving away on Freecycle. You can find some many treasures for your house, and you can make simple alterations to them to freshen them up, like using some chalk paint or adding new handles.

224.   Come up with interests that you can centre around your home. Grow plants, feed the birds and birdwatch, stargaze at night.

225.   Whenever you feel the urge to go shopping, make a list of all the negatives that come from being a consumer.

226.   Read books that encourage a frugal mindset. Read books on the Great Depression, the Second World War and rationing, etc. You will feel rich by comparison, and it will remind you of what's truly important in life.

227.   Stop buying cheap tat. It's tempting to buy things just because they are cheap, or because they suit a particular season, but they aren't made to last and it's a waste of your money. It's better to invest in one solid piece rather than in lots of pieces of what will quickly become rubbish.

228.   Slow down and enjoy the things in life that you never take the time to notice. Look out the window, watch the rain and feel happy that you're dry inside.

229.   Look for things you loved to do as a kid. Go for a walk in the rain and walk through puddles in your wellies, bake messy buns and overdo the icing and sprinkles, do some printing using random objects and paint to cheer you up.

230.   Go beach combing. It's a free activity and you get so much from it. You can find lots of living things in rockpools and you might come across some amazing shells or even a fossil.

231.   Make themed days in your household. It helps to turn what would just be an ordinary day into something special. For example, have an Autumn day: collect leaves, go for crunchy leaf walks, light scented candles, bake a loaf or cake, draw some autumnal pictures to decorate the walls. You can come up with any theme you like.

232.   If you can't afford to get wall art for your house, frame your own art or your children's. You can get very cheap frames from somewhere like Ikea and create a display on your wall for very little money.

233.   Don't buy expensive crafting supplies for your kids. Use what you already have. Give them empty packaging to paint and draw on. Let them draw on the ground with chalk and take photos of their masterpieces. I find that whenever I take pictures of my kids' artwork, it makes them feel special because they know I want to save it forever, even if the rain will wash it away an hour later.

234.   Look out for activity books for your kids. You can often find them in charity shops with only one page completed and the rest of the book blank. They keep their minds active and they don't cost a lot.

235.   Look in every section of a charity shop. People tend to skip sections that don't interest them, but when you look everywhere, you can find some hidden treasures.

236.   Google free events in your nearest city. There are probably plenty of venues you don't know about that don't charge entry fees.

237.   Find out about the free art exhibitions in your area. There are often smaller exhibitions for emerging artists that don't charge anything.

238.   Keep a diary of your simplest adventures. Stick in pictures and mementos to make you take the time to appreciate how much you already have.

239.   Stop bringing souvenirs home from all your adventures. Bring memories and photos with you instead.

240.   Host a clothing exchange, or a kitchen exchange, or whatever kind of exchange you like. Get new items for free and clear out unused ones at the same time without spending a penny.

241.   Consider shopping for good quality, cheap items and reselling them for a little more.

242.   Pet sit to make some extra cash and to get to spend some time with animals without the cost of having a pet.

243.   Spend time weeding your garden. It's time consuming and grounding and you will be surprised by how many ideas come to you while you're doing it. It's a free activity that will improve your mood and the appearance of your garden.

244.   If you live in a flat, create a windowsill herb garden or grow tomatoes or strawberries in a sunny spot. You can also put certain

vegetables in water when used, let them sprout and then cut from them or replant them.

245. Look out for quirky, free events. They might not always be widely advertised, so you will have to look around. Look out for flyers, read free local papers or research online.

246. Consider anything a win whenever you manage not to spend money doing it. Congratulate yourself and give yourself the incentive to keep going.

247. Make a no spend diary. Document the waves of your emotions, the feelings of withdrawal you might get from not spending and the overall feeling of achievement at the end.

248. Go to the library and search for books on simple living, gratitude and budgeting. Work on changing your mindset and the numbers will follow.

249. Switch off everything you aren't using. If you have kids, train them to turn off lights, the TV and music whenever they aren't using them. If you're drying your clothes in the tumble dryer, remove your delicates and hang them to dry first, so they don't get destroyed. It will cut down on drying time and make your garments last longer too.

250. Don't buy fancy cleaning products or specific products for specific jobs. Get some bleach, some antibacterial spray and some cloths and save the money you would have wasted on different products that all do the same job.

251. Don't go into shops to browse (unless you don't have your purse or wallet with you.) Browsing always turns into buying.

252. Attend to small inconveniences before they become big problems. Fixing a small leak is much easier than fixing rotten floors and holes in ceilings.

253.   Don't get a credit card. Buy what you have already budgeted for or save for things you would like. Don't get into unnecessary debt or pay unnecessary interest.

254.   Choose your friends carefully. Don't spend time with people with hugely different values to you. Your friends often influence your behaviour. If you spend a lot of time with people that are seeking a certain lifestyle, you will find yourself trying to emulate them.

255.   Make your own pizza dough and your own sauce in bulk and freeze what you aren't using that day. It means you will be less inclined to get takeaway, because you know you can pull something delicious out of the freezer and there is minimal preparation involved.

256.   Spend time doing things like organising your books. These types of activities are free, but you still get a sense of satisfaction from completing them. You will benefit from the improved look of your surroundings too.

257.   Research activities before you pay for them. Read the reviews or ask around to see if they are worth doing. There is no point in paying large amounts of money for activities you won't enjoy or that barely last an hour.

258.   Plan ahead. Reserve money for treats. If you don't do this, you will feel deprived, but if you factor it into your budget, you will still feel rewarded without breaking your budget.

259.   If you have a treat that means a lot to you, instead of depriving yourself of it, make up for it in another area. I know I love going out for coffee, so I keep my food budget at a particular number each week. We still have a varied and rich diet, but I'd rather "waste" some money on coffee shops and getting a change of environment to write in than on extra food items that will go uneaten or more expensive branded foods that taste no different to us.

260.   Add new recipes to your repertoire. Look up recipes online or watch YouTube videos to change things up in your house. I find that I am most tempted to order takeaway or eat out when I'm bored with what I'm making or eating or whenever something sounds unappealing because it's become too repetitive.

261.   Learn how to make your favourite takeaways at home. Allow more money for special ingredients for that particular night rather than spending much more on food you order from a restaurant.

262.   Combine car journeys. Instead of running lots of separate errands, think of the ones that are close together and consolidate them to save money on petrol.

263.   Keep your petrol tank around the half-full mark. It is more economical, wastes less fuel and it means you won't get caught out with an empty tank either.

264.   Try to replace bad money habits with healthier ones. When you feel like walking around, do it in a park or a pretty place in nature rather than in a shopping centre or in town. Walk different routes to avoid places that tempt you.

265.   Whenever you are eating out, look out for offers. There are many places that serve coffee or tea and allow you to add a donut for an extra pound. Read the menu before you order and make note of the best deals.

266.   Avoid buying drinks with fancy names in coffee shops or in bars. They are often dressed up versions of the same drink. For example, you can get a fancy praline hot chocolate with whipped cream and chopped nuts and it's £4.50 because it's their seasonal addition to the menu. You can just order a hot chocolate with hazelnut syrup and achieve the same effect at a reduced rate.

267.   Use your rewards. Use your Clubcard vouchers. Make sure you convert them into vouchers to double the points and get the most value out of them. Browse the options in your area. You can often use them for a meal out or a cinema date. It's easy to forget about them when you're busy and you're shopping in different places, but they do add up.

268.   Get rewards apps on your phone. It means you won't have to perform a ten-minute long search in the shop, only to find out you left your card in the house. You can get discounts in many stores. Boots Advantage card and The Works are a couple of examples of rewards schemes that offer good discounts.

269.   Buy multipacks of chocolate and sweets instead of individual bars and packets. They are usually much better value and there isn't a huge difference. If you find them smaller, it is still cheaper to eat two from a multipack than one larger one from the individual bars shelf!

270.   Practise the art of going without. I think people are afraid to do without things they think they need. Sometimes, we need to strip back to basics to remember what we really do need and what we could afford to cut back on.

271.   Only buy toiletries in discount shops and cheaper pharmacies. There have been so many times in the past whenever I have bought toiletries and make-up at full price, only to see them later that week for a quarter of the price. Don't go to the obvious places first. Look for the independent pharmacies and the Savers in your area.

272.   Consider ordering items you typically buy in person online. It cuts out the temptation to add additional items to the basket, as you can be more targeted about what you're shopping for. You won't get lured in by fancy window displays or end of aisle displays either.

273.   If you see the word "offer," don't automatically assume it is a real offer. Compare the price to own brand items and the same

product in another store. Don't take the word of the retailer as the deciding factor on whether something is a true offer.

274.   Buy pieces of clothing that you can rotate, and wear paired with different things. Think about the items in your wardrobe that you have worn the most. They are usually staple items, like a pinafore or a top that go with everything. You can always change outfits up with whatever you choose to pair with them.

275.   Buy good quality shoes. It's better to invest in a pair and only need to replace them once every few years than to buy cheap and not so cheerful ones that fall apart after a week.

276.   Take note whenever you feel unhappy and whenever you feel the urge to overspend. Pay attention to your triggers and try to find replacements that make you feel good but that don't require you to spend money.

277.   Don't go shopping whenever you're bored, tired, emotional or hungry.

278.   Bake your own bread. It is so easy to make and very therapeutic. If you have a kitchen aid or a mixer with a dough hook, you don't even have to knead it. I recently found a no knead recipe for bread that works so well. It just needs to rise for longer and you can put it straight into the oven. There are so many simple bread recipes online and you can add whatever extra ingredients you like to them to make them more interesting.

279.   Don't immediately throw out fruit or vegetables that look past their best. Think about how you could use them up. You can cut off the bruised parts and use the rest to make soups, stews, fruit pies and crumbles, jams, coulis and smoothies.

280.   Keep your life as clutter-free as you can. It will make you much more focused and streamlined in general. The less stuff you have to tidy up, the more time you have to do the things you enjoy.

281.   Don't buy anything because it is good value; buy it because you truly want or need it.

282.   This might sound painfully obvious, but it is often overlooked: don't buy anything you can't afford.

283.   Think about the things that people did for entertainment in the past and bring them back into regular usage. People didn't have the same disposable income then, or the same access to shops, but they managed to lead rich lives.

284.   Consider dumpster diving if you live near an accessible one. You might uncover lots of treasures that would have just gone to landfill.

285.   Cut back on the number of devices in your house. The less you use them, the less electricity you waste, the less money you spend on games and apps and the more time you have for other forms of productivity.

286.   Check for discounted fruit and veg boxes in supermarkets. Some shops have started to put together boxes of fruit and veg that are on the point of expiring. They are still perfectly good to cook with and to eat but they are just marked as best before that date.

287.   Don't sign up for expensive gym memberships. Consider paying as you go for a gym or a swimming pool – it might work out cheaper if you're only going once a week.

288.   Whenever you're out and about, keep your eyes open and look out for local events that are advertised on posters and banners.

289. Get rid of one item each time you buy something new. By implementing this practice, it will make you much more thoughtful about what you do bring into your house, because you will know you also have to get rid of something else.

290. Hold a garage sale or a yard sale, even if they aren't popular in your area. You'll be surprised by the number of people that stop by out of curiosity, and people love to find bargains. You might start a new trend in your neighbourhood.

291. Look up recipes online for things you wouldn't think to make yourself. Make your own coffee syrup, make your own vegetable stock and make your own tea blends. It will help you to use up odds and ends too.

292. Create your own compost. Look up videos on how to do it online. Save your food scraps and coffee grounds and turn them into nourishing soil for your plants.

293. Invest in a glue gun. You can use it for so many craft projects and to do simple repairs.

294. Take up knitting or crochet and develop a skill that allows you to make blankets and other warm, useful items.

295. Get a slow cooker and use it to make big batches of meals. Freeze some for a quick dinner another night.

296. Put all your vegetable cuttings into a freezer bag and gather them until you have enough to make stock or gravy.

297. Consider making your own versions of cheap recipes instead of automatically buying them. It's so easy to make pancakes, potato bread, Yorkshire puddings and no bake treats.

298.   Save any old fabrics for other purposes. For example, don't throw out an old T-shirt. You can cut it up and use the pieces in other projects or use them as cloths for cleaning the house. You can turn old shirts, etc into napkins by cutting them up and stitching a simple border around the outside of them.

299.   Host simple coffee afternoons or dinner parties with friends and spend much less than you would in a café or restaurant. Even if you buy a packet of buns, it will probably cost less than a cup of coffee and a single bun in a café would.

300.   Make things last as long as possible. You don't have to buy a new sofa every time yours gets tired looking. Just add a pretty throw and some cushions and bring it back to life again. People barely replaced anything in the past and they just made it work. Changing furniture all the time is a modern thing and a bit like fast fashion.

301.   If you are fed up with the look of your home, go to Ikea and get a few simple, cheap items to change the feel of it. It's amazing how much a new shelf or a mirror can change a room.

302.   Don't allow yourself to get bored. Listen to a podcast, download some books from Libby, go to the library and browse for some books. Pick up some crafting or cookery books while you're there. If your mind and hands aren't idle, you don't have time to think about shopping. Use the library computers for a change of scenery if you're getting bored working at your own desk.

303.   Limit your subscriptions. Don't have several streaming services at once. Rotate them if you want to watch different things. Have Netflix for a month, Disney Plus for a month, etc.

304.   Don't keep extras of everything. If you have too many of a particular item, you won't remember where you put it or remember to use it anyway.

305.   Have a well filled spice rack. If you have an array of spices and herbs in your kitchen, it's easier to create flavourful meals, which makes eating out less tempting. If you can cook better at home, you will want to eat at home more often.

306.   Use fewer products. Think about the amount of shower gel you use, or the amount of toothpaste. Is it the right amount, or would it make any difference to use slightly less?

307.   Make use of the land you have and keep trees and plants that produce fruit and veg (if you're good at growing them!) If you aren't confident in your ability to do this, start small and work up to more complicated tasks.

308.   Find ways to change your look without spending money. If you're feeling bored, you don't necessarily need an expensive haircut. You can look up videos online of hair tutorials for your specific hair type or you can dye it at home or do simple haircuts yourself.

309.   Make gifts at home. People will appreciate the thought you've put into them, and you might be the only person they know that handmakes their gift, which is special and memorable.

310.   Look out for offers online. Follow places you enjoy visiting on Facebook and Instagram so you can keep up to date with their events and reduced prices. Sometimes businesses release tickets for a short time, for example, the National Trust put a set number of free passes up and the first people to sign up get to visit for free.

311.   Consider staying at home instead of going on holiday. Pick a few activities you love to do that you don't often get to do. You'll still feel like you've spoilt yourself but at a fraction of the price.

312.   Take up camping if it's something that has always interested you. After you have bought all the supplies, there is just a pitching fee and you have somewhere cheap to stay.

313.   Spend time learning how to do things yourself so you don't have to pay others to do them for you. Don't rush anything. Make sure you slow down and learn how to do something properly instead of racing through it, making mistakes and losing confidence in yourself.

314.   Don't agree to do things you can't afford just because of social pressure. If someone is a true friend, they will stick around anyway.

315.   If you really want to read a book, see if the library can order it in for you first. They will happily order books for you for a small fee, which might work out cheaper than buying the book yourself.

316.   Turn everything off at the wall when you go to bed at night or whenever you aren't using them. It will save on electricity and make your home safer fire-safety wise too.

317.   Consider growing plants and selling them. If you're good at something, sell it and be proud of it.

318.   Sell unused kitchen appliances. You'd be surprised by how much money you can get for them.

319.   Sign up to apps like Too Good to Go. Shop late at night whenever you can to get the food that is discounted at the end of the day.

320.   Reuse things like kitchen foil and freezer bags if they have just been used for something like cookies or bread. The smallest things can make a big difference to your budget.

321.   Stop buying snacks and make your own. Buy full sized bags instead of treat-sized ones.

322.   Start only carrying cash. It's harder to spend it whenever you see it in front of you and once it runs out, don't allow yourself to withdraw any more.

323.   Start putting back items you don't love. Be honest with yourself; if you have to stop and think about whether to buy something, you don't really want or need it.

324.   Find other functions for items you already have at home. For example, you don't need a scarf hanger; you can just loop them around a regular hanger. I recently realised I had left my garden trowel behind in my last house. Instead of running out to buy one, I just looked for another utensil I could use in the meantime. It might be nice to buy a shoe rack, but in the meantime, a box will do.

325.   Make full use of your memberships. Don't save them for special occasions. Go on a Friday afternoon if you aren't working or make it a habit to visit at the weekend. You don't have to stay for a full day out; you can call in for an hour, have a walk around and go home.

326.   Look for Woodland Trust forests in your region. They are free to visit and quiet because they aren't as well advertised as the National Trust or other places that charge entry.

327.   Visit all the libraries within walking or driving distance in your area. Ask for their events programme and find out if there are classes you'd like to attend. They often host one-off events for kids too. We have attended movie afternoons, bedtime story evenings, visits from the fire service, craft days, writing groups and Lego workshops.

328.   Buy digital prints from artists online or cut images from magazines, etc and frame them yourself. It's cheaper than buying ready-framed prints.

329.   Stop chronic snacking (I am definitely guilty of this!) Eat more satisfying meals and try to break the habit of constant snacking between meals.

330.   Go through your bank statements and notice the payments that make you feel guilty – those are probably the areas you need to stop spending in the most.

331.   Every time you make a payment, round it up to the nearest pound and transfer the pennies into savings. They will very quickly add up.

332.   Buy less food for your household. Think about how much you throw away. Make your grocery budget as tiny as you possibly can. Consider changing your shopping habits. Shop less frequently and plan better before you go. Take inventory of what you already have.

333.   Use apps like Supercook to help you come up with recipes whenever you feel like you have little left to work with.

334.   Don't rule out foodbanks. If you are really struggling, they exist for a reason. You can always donate to them whenever you're in a better financial position. You don't have to feel bad for accepting the help that is on offer when you need it.

335.   Get a cheaper phone contract. Keep your paid off phone if it is still working whenever you have paid off your contract and change to pay as you go.

336.   Shop around for cheaper insurance. Change suppliers annually after you have done your research. Few insurers pay more for your loyalty. They usually rely on you renewing your insurance with them out of laziness and to save yourself the bother of looking around, but it's amazing how much money you can save yourself just by spending a little time doing this.

337.   Keep frozen fruit and veg in your freezer. It doesn't spoil like fresh products, and you can quickly whip up meals and snacks with it. Throw frozen berries into muffin mix, make fruit pies, make smoothies and frozen yogurt lollies, fry frozen veg in a little butter for quick preparation and great flavour.

338.   Save jars if you have the space to store them. You can use them for making your own jams and chutneys. They are so easy to make, and you just have to sterilise the jars. There is plenty of information available online about how to do this.

339.   Have a clear-out and sell your items online or at a car boot sale. One person's trash really is another person's treasure. I've been to car boot sales, and I've seen people buying the most random things. Don't assume everything you don't want isn't wanted by others.

340.   If you have a skill, enter a contest and challenge yourself to win. There are often cash prizes.

341.   Consider downsizing. Do you need to live in the house you have? Do you have lots of extra rooms? Consider running an Airbnb from the spare room. You can make lots of extra money doing this.

342.   Buy items for £1 and resell them for £2. It can be fun looking for little treasures that someone will love and making a small profit on them.

343.   Don't waste money on parking in the city centre; carpool or use park and rides instead.

344.   Go for bikes rides with your family. It's a feel-good activity that keeps everyone busy and occupied and you can research the best places to go for bike rides in your area. There might be cycle paths or trails you can explore. Bring a flask and some sandwiches with you and make a day out of it.

345.   Bring bags with you every time you go out. Keep some in your car or in your handbag. If you don't, you'll end up wasting so much money on buying bags. The kind the fold up into a small bag are handy to keep in your backpack.

346.   Make your own mini pizzas. It's a fun way to have a pizza party and very cheap. You just need dough, cheese, sauce and a few toppings for people to choose. It's a great way to entertain kids too.

347.   Make items from scratch that you tend to buy without thinking about it. Make your own tortillas, soda bread, potato bread, etc.

348.   Buy simple appliances to make your food more exciting. They don't have to be expensive. Get an own-brand toastie machine or a hand blender. Think about cost per use. If you use it all the time and it helps you to eat at home more often, it is worth purchasing.

349.   Create an outdoor space for yourself that's like a little veranda to sit on. You don't need a lot of space to do it. You can create a corner in your garden, a spot on a balcony or even a seating area beside your front step. Get a small, cheap table and chairs from Ikea and dress it up with fairy lights, bunting and bird houses. Make it a tranquil and inspiring area to work or relax in.

350.   Create different areas within a room. Make an office corner for you to work in. Place it in front of a window or in front of a noticeboard with inspiring pictures covering it. Make a reading nook with a comfortable chair, a shelf for your books and a lamp. Create areas related to your hobbies and your work. Use items you already have around the house and add small touches from charity shops and discount stores.

351.   Shop in places like TK Maxx or outlets. They have great quality, branded clothing with huge reductions.

352.   Only buy items that add value to your life. Ask yourself that question before you make a purchase: what value will this add to my life? If you can't answer the question, put it back.

353.   Just because you like something, it doesn't mean you have to own it. You can look at something, appreciate its beauty and then leave it for someone else to enjoy. The novelty of a new purchase usually wears off after a couple of uses anyway.

354.   Notice the cycle of trying to satisfy yourself with material items.

355.   Don't immediately throw out free local papers. Sometimes "junk mail" contains hidden treasure. I have got lots of coffee vouchers from them, as well as a removals company that was much cheaper than any I might have found online.

356.   Think of alternative ways of doing things. If you want to create art, what do you already have on hand to work with at home? Can you paint on a different surface? Can you use your kids' art supplies? Do you really need to go to the shop to get started?

357.   Avoid taking out loans for things you can live without. It just creates more financial pressure that you don't need, and that takes the joy out of the purchase.

358.   Don't take on any new commitments you can't afford. If the thought of something makes you feel stressed, it isn't right for you.

359.   Go for a less obvious option if you are doing something like organising a birthday party. Phone local community centres and see if they hire rooms. Don't go for the most expensive option just because it's the first thing you think of.

360.   Don't put all your money into entering the lottery, playing instant games or entering paying competitions. If you look at the odds,

you have a very slim chance of winning anything significant. Put the money you would have spent on tickets into a savings account instead.

361.　Use wax melts rather than candles to scent your home. They last longer and you can get them much cheaper than candles. You just need a wax burner and some tealights. You can also scent your home with cinnamon sticks and star anise, etc simmering in water. Use your cooking to scent your home too. Baking bread produces a lovely scent that lingers for a long time afterwards.

362.　If someone you know is getting rid of stuff, ask if you can have a look first. You might find a use for the things that they have deemed clutter.

363.　If your kids have lots of broken crayons, take the wrappers off and mix the colours in muffin tins. Melt them in the oven to make large marbled crayons. Reserve a muffin tin for this as it will probably stain it.

364.　Go to shops like The Works whenever they have a sale on and stock up on presents for any birthdays throughout the year. They usually have something that will appeal to everyone, and their discounts are amazing.

365.　Buy greetings cards in bulk. Go to a card shop and buy the ten for £10 cards. Get a variety of them so you have some to suit different people. If you have kids, this is useful for whenever you receive lots of invites to birthday parties.

366.　Buy discounted box mixes from the baking section in supermarkets. If you buy the own brand ones (usually on the shelves closest to the floor,) it is less expensive than buying all the ingredients to bake your own. Just add whatever ingredients you like and easily make batches of cookies and cakes. It's much cheaper than buying shop bought ones.

367.   If you enjoy doing something but you think you do it too often, and it's becoming costly, it's better to cut down to doing it once a week instead. You don't have to cut it out entirely. It's better to keep it as something to look forward to. Don't deprive yourself of it entirely or you'll be more likely to splurge to make up for the loss.

368.   Take the lid off toiletries to get out the last of them. It might seem like an insignificant amount, but if extends the time you can go without buying new ones, it's worth doing. Adding on an extra week or two to each bottle makes a significant difference over time.

369.   If you use lipstick, use a lipstick brush to use up whatever is left inside the holder when it's finished.

370.   Do crafts with your kids that don't involve spending huge amounts of money. My kids always lose interest in everything after about fifteen minutes anyway, so there is no point in buying lots of expensive materials for a short activity.

371.   Get your kids to help with things. It keeps them busy, and they learn lots of new, useful skills. Mine have been helping me at car boot sales recently and they have been enjoying meeting new people and counting the money in their jar!

372.   Read as often as you possibly can. It's a cheap hobby, it keeps your mind and hands busy, and you gain so much from it without spending a lot of money.

373.   Change your furniture around. It will give your home a new look and make you less inclined to go out as often for a change of scenery. (I need to try this!)

374.   Think about the activities your grandparents did and model your life on theirs. They probably filled their time with valuable pursuits that didn't cost a lot of money. There were fewer options

available then, so people had to be more imaginative and more easily satisfied.

375.   Make breakfasts in bulk. If they are ready to go, you'll be less likely to pick something up on your way to work. You can prep overnight oats and keep them in the fridge for the following morning. I like to top mine with frozen berries so they defrost overnight and become like a coulis on top of your oats. Make pancakes or waffles in advance so you can quickly reheat them in the toaster. Don't overcomplicate things in the morning. Have your coffee maker set up and ready to go.

376.   Use your slow cooker when you can't be bothered to cook. Just shove ingredients in it and allow it to create one pot meals for you that are magically ready by dinnertime. If you brown the meat beforehand and add some flour, it will produce more flavour and a thicker sauce.

377.   Don't immediately throw out stale food. Put crisps in the oven to crisp them up again, use cracker crumbs in meatloaf or in meatballs and use bread to make croutons or breadcrumbs to top oven dishes.

378.   Use battery lights and candles before you turn on electric lamps. Fill your home with fairy lights or cheap candles. Just make sure you put the candles away from fabric, etc.

379.   Try to go out and not spend any money and see if you feel any different by the end of the day. Do you remember what you might have been tempted to buy? Do you feel like you've lost out? Or do you feel proud of yourself and more grateful for what you already have?

380.   Go to council run events with free entry. They often give away freebies too. We were lucky enough to get a free recipe book, kids' books and some cooking utensils from the Autumn fair.

381.   Don't waste money on fancy versions of things when you can get cheap ones that are just as good. My favourite perfume is one that I got from Primark. I have one from years ago that was about fifty pounds that I got with a voucher and it's no better than that one.

382.   Buy second hand furniture. It is often stronger and better made than newer furniture anyway. Give it a clean-up and it will be as good as new.

383.   Spend your time making things rather than consuming things. Creativity is even more addictive than buying things. The more you do it, the more time you'll want to spend producing new things.

384.   Turn free activities into something special. Sharing the simplest things with your family can make the best memories. For example, my kids love going out to collect blossom, or conkers, depending on the season, or shells! They love hunting for them and filling their pockets with them and they often reminisce about the times we've done that in the past.

385.   Start journalling. It is a cheap activity that is very rewarding, it's like free therapy and it helps you to come up with so many ideas. Every few months, you can "invest" in a new journal you love too.

386.   Don't base your outings around the weather. Go out for a wintery walk and wrap up warm. Walk on the beach in the rain and have a hot bath after you get home. Endure the weather and reward yourself with a hot drink after. It will make you appreciate the warmth even more and most activities in nature are free of charge.

387.   If your oven is turned on, make sure it's worthwhile. Whenever you can, double up on the meals you're making, make bread or bake at the same time. It means you aren't using lots of electricity making everything separately.

388.   If you're letting something simmer, instead of having the cooker on the whole time, turn it off, leave the pot on the heated ring and cover the top with tin foil and a lid to keep the heat in. It will continue to cook for quite a long time.

389.   Make your own decorations. Make paper chains and paper snowflakes for Christmas, painted eggs for Easter and hand-painted banners for birthdays. You can get rolls of paper in discount shops or just stick pages together. Add a balloon to a chair and put a fancy place setting at the head of the table, look up how to fold napkins in a fancy way. You don't have to buy disposable decorations; just work with what you have. People remember how they felt on a particular occasion; not the specific decorations they were surrounded by.

390.   Give your kids chalk and get them to draw around shadows on the ground. They can use found objects or their own shadows. Draw funny faces on them.

391.   Plant sprouted potatoes in your garden. You will have to be patient, but they will grow into new potato plants. Whenever they have grown into full sized plants, dig them up to find your homegrown potatoes underneath.

392.   Make a fairy garden in a plant pot. It's an easy project for adults and kids. Just get some pretty shells or stones, a plant and some pieces of wood and be as imaginative as you like. You can cheaply buy a fairy, or you can make your own with a wooden peg and some fabric.

393.   Make objects out of lolly sticks. All you need are some lolly sticks which you can buy cheaply in the pound shop or a craft shop and glue them together. Paint your constructions whenever you're finished making them.

394.   See what materials you can find in a charity shop or at a car boot sale to turn into something else. There are usually some unwanted craft supplies hidden away. Work with what you find and

see what you can come up with. Sometimes great ideas are born out of limited resources.

395.   Buy foods that are versatile. Oats can be made into lots of different things – you can have porridge, oatmeal cookies, granola, cereal bars, banana and oat flapjacks. Peanut butter can be used in a hundred different ways too. Stock up on foods that have many different uses and can be used for different meals.

396.   Look for cheaper versions of expensive ingredients in recipes. You don't need risotto rice; just use long grain rice in the same way. You don't need shallots; just use an onion. The cheapest bars of chocolate are great for baking, as are the cheapest boxes of cereal.

397.   Think about how you can fix something before you throw it away. Thinking that way helps you to become more resourceful and you develop skills that you will use time and again.

398.   Have a good skincare regime but use cheap cleanser and moisturiser. It doesn't matter how expensive it is; sometimes the simplest products work the best and the habit of looking after your skin every day is the most important thing.

399.   Visit places that are less popular. Go to a town you don't know at all and uncover what is there. It can be a fun adventure even whenever you don't find anything lifechanging. Most towns have a playground for kids, a place to walk in nature and a coffee shop. Sometimes you just need a change of scenery, and going somewhere that is less popular is a cheaper option, and it's less busy too.

400.   Look for restaurants outside cities. Some of the best restaurants I have eaten in have been in the middle of the countryside, in old inn types of buildings. They serve big portions of hearty food, and they don't charge the prices that city restaurants do.

401.   Make time to rest. Your body needs it, and we are taught that we should constantly be running around in our society, but doing so is costly both to our health and our finances.

402.   Get the cheapest broadband deal that you can find that has a fast speed. If you go for the cheapest available option, it will probably be so slow and basic that you will go out all the time to find faster wifi. Find a good balance between price and a speed that serves your needs as a household.

403.   Wait until off season to upgrade your home. Buy garden furniture at the end of the summer and Christmas lights in January. The prices will be much more reasonable, and you can use them for years to come.

404.   Everyone seems to love air fryers at the moment. We have a deep fryer, and it makes chips that taste like they came straight from a restaurant or chip shop. Having some appliances that aren't classed "essential" can make you feel like your home is more luxurious. Buy yourself the donut maker if it means you make fewer visits to Tim Hortons!

405.   Don't feel the pressure to keep up with modern traditions. No one needed an Elf on the Shelf or a Christmas Eve box until 2018 and everyone got by fine without them. Giving kids too many gifts just make them view everything as disposable and easily replaceable anyway.

406.   Make cookies from scratch and ice and decorate them. It's good for the soul, kids love it, and it fills a slow afternoon. There's something very grounding about making your own baked goods and you get to enjoy them with a cup of tea when you're finished.

407.   Buy own brand spirits. I have never noticed a difference in taste, and there can be a twenty-pound difference between a bottle of branded and unbranded alcohol.

408.   Look in your fridge for any fruit or vegetables languishing in the bottom drawer. Google recipes using those ingredients and use up all the scraps that will otherwise end up in the bin.

409.   Get a chest freezer. It might cost money and take up a bit of space, but you'll have so much storage space and it will make it much easier to plan ahead with meals and cook in bulk.

410.   You don't need to buy new things all the time. We have had the same towels and sheets for years. Sometimes, we get a new set, but the old ones work just fine. Regularly replacing everything is a modern, throwaway mindset. My parents gave me some bed sheets a couple of years ago from whenever we were teenagers that were still in good condition.

411.   Whenever you get a gift voucher or money as a present, put it aside for a day whenever you need a pick-me-up and don't spend it straight away just for the sake of it.

412.   Challenge yourself to read a book a week, or once a month from the library. Going to get a new book is a lovely ritual and having a deadline makes you much more likely to read it. Create a reading challenge for yourself on Goodreads.

413.   Spend your time leaving reviews for products, books and crafts you have purchased. It's hugely helpful to other buyers and gives the sellers a boost too.

414.   If you are selling anything online, don't be tempted to browse too. Just upload your items and get off the site asap!

415.   Don't immediately say yes to everything your kids ask for. Save treats for certain days so it is recognised as a treat and appreciated.

416.   Get school uniforms from school sales and check if your area has a uniform recycling scheme. I dropped off some uniforms my kids were finished with this year and got some new ones too.

417.   Consider having advertising on your car. You can display an ad on your car for a particular company and they will pay you for advertising for them.

418.   Bring your own snacks and drinks to the cinema. Contrary to popular belief, it isn't against the rules, and no one will scold you for it. Whenever you have just spent twenty pounds on tickets, there's no point in spending the same amount again on snacks.

419.   Have a place for everything and keep like with like. It makes it much less frustrating to navigate your home and find your possessions. Otherwise, so much time is wasted in looking for items. (I'm speaking from personal experience!)

420.   Set a weekly grocery limit and make sure you don't go over it. Use a calculator as you shop if it helps.

421.   Give yourself a weekly allowance and challenge yourself to keep as much of the money as you can. You can put it into a collection for something much more worthwhile than all the tiny, easily forgotten purchases you would have made instead.

422.   Set up selling accounts on eBay, Depop, Etsy, Vinted or any other sites you feel drawn to. Make it a regular practice to clear out the items you aren't using.

423.   Don't allow yourself to be guilted into signing up for charities. Give freely when you can and to the causes that matter to you, but don't allow financial obligations to come from unexpected and unplanned sources.

424.   Review your direct debit payments regularly and see what you can cut. There will almost always be something you aren't using that you've forgotten about.

425.   Gladly accept any freebies that come your way. Even if you don't have a use for them, you can give them to someone else that does, or you can sell them to make some extra cash.

426.   If you want to bring back the excitement of going out to pick a video from the shop on a Friday night, go to a charity shop and get some DVD's for 50p to £1. Whenever you're finished with them, donate them again.

427.   Keep a good supply of microwave popcorn in your cupboard so you can have an impromptu movie night any time you feel like it.

428.   Make a list of all the things that make you feel rich that don't involve spending money and keep it handy for whenever you run out of ideas or get budgeting fatigue.

429.   If you need curtains but you can't afford the cost of getting them made to fit, buy second hand curtains or cheap fabric from IKEA and alter them to make them the right size.

430.   Do rock painting with positive pictures and messages on them and spend a day with your kids scattering them on the beach. They will cheer up whoever happens to find them.

431.   Buy cheap diffusers to give your home an expensive, hotel-like scent.

432.   Play music in your home to create an appealing ambience. If you have Alexa, create an "everywhere" group on the app so it plays throughout the house while you are moving from room to room.

433.   Get a pop-up greenhouse. You can buy them cheaply and you assemble them like a tent. It means you can grow plants that require a warmer climate to grow well, but without the cost of a greenhouse.

434.   If you're feeling deprived and feel the urge to shop, go out intentionally to buy one thing. It is much better than buying a whole collection of items and it will satisfy your need to shop without breaking the bank.

435.   Find a simple muffin mix online and make up the dry mix in bulk. You can use it whenever you like and make different additions to it, like frozen berries, chocolate, raisins, etc.

436.   Don't go to every event that's on expecting not to spend money. Most days out involve a certain amount of spending. Plan and budget for them instead of going along, assuming it won't cost anything.

437.   Don't buy anything you didn't plan to buy just because it's on offer – unless you know you will use it soon.

438.   Regularly go through cupboards and storage boxes in your home. You'll be surprised by what you find there. Each time I do this, I find something I thought we had run out of or that I just forgot I bought.

439.   Don't spend money on salons, hairdressers or dry cleaners. Find alternative ways to do the same jobs at home. With the right tools and some research, it's easy to do these things for yourself.

440.   Buy matinee tickets for the cinema. They are cheaper than tickets sold in the evening and our local cinema does a matinee snack special: popcorn, a drink and some sweets for £3.

441.   Whenever a bag for life bursts, you can return it to a bag for life provider and get a new one.

442.   Eat recommended portion sizes. Overeating is extremely common in our society. If we just pay attention to our portion sizes, it makes a huge difference to our food budget.

443.   Keep dessert for special days. You don't need to make it every night and it was designed to be a treat. It's easy to fall into a trap of providing your kids with a treat after every meal, but they really don't need it, and it's healthier for them not to have one as often.

444.   Keep your home clean so you can relax in it. It's hard to relax whenever you're staring at the physical manifestation of your to-do list.

445.   Keep jars whenever you're finished with them and use them for storage and to make your own chutneys, jams, pickles, etc.

446.   Make food as gifts for people you know. You can make cookie mixes, trail mix, or even dog biscuits. Just add a pretty ribbon and you have a lovely, personalised gift.

447.   Get into recycling. It's a great interest to cultivate and it helps you to become more conscious of the areas in which you are wasting your own money too.

448.   Get involved in a park run, in raising money for charity or in a beach or park clean-up. These are all low-cost activities that are very rewarding.

449.   Make your own cordial or mulled wine in a slow cooker. It's an easy way to use up fruit that is turning brown, to get a homemade, warming drink and to scent your home.

450.   Start using the eco cycle on your washing machine. It might take longer, but it does use less energy. I learned this tip from my sister.

451.   Use up all your leftovers. If you don't feel like eating the same meal twice, turn it into something else. Take inspiration from your favourite restaurant meals.

452.   Talk about frugality with others. Pick up tips you mightn't have heard about otherwise. Most people like to find ways to save money. It doesn't have to be a forbidden conversational topic.

453.   Apply for the Amazon shopper panel and get rewards whenever you complete short surveys. You might have to join the waiting list, but you will get approved and save a couple of pounds a month on Amazon.

454.   Start a jar for loose change. Whenever it is filled, take it to the bank or to a Coinstar and treat yourself.

455.   Buy generic brands of medication. It does the exact same job, but it can be a tenth of the price. Don't pay extra just for a recognisable name. If the pharmacy is selling it, it's safe to use.

456.   Put expensive holidays on hold. You can always go abroad in the future whenever you have more money available. Book a local Airbnb either very far in advance or very last minute if you want to get a good deal. If you find somewhere close to home, you only have to pay for the accommodation – not for the travel. Some accommodation accepts Tesco Clubcard vouchers too.

457.   Use borrowing libraries. I have seen lots of these in small towns and inside major supermarkets. You just borrow a book, leave one in its place and repeat the process once you've finished reading it. The same thing exists for tools and all kinds of other items if you just do some research.

458.   Encourage your kids to appreciate the simple things in life. My kids love nature and finding unusual things outside. My daughter was

very excited to find an acorn the other day and we made a little display of conkers and acorns. If you help them to notice the little things and set an example in that way, they will find joy in the things that money can't buy.

459.   Stop putting yourself in debt over Christmas. It's one day out of 365 days and it's the same every year. Ask yourself if you can remember the details of last Christmas and the items you bought then. If you can't, was it worth putting yourself under financial strain for it?

460.   Create your own values and stick to them. Don't be swayed by what other people are doing because our priorities are all completely different. Striving to keep up with another person's values will never make you happy because we all have different desires in our hearts.

461.   If you regularly use public transport, do some research to find the cheapest monthly or annual pass.

462.   Stop using carparks that charge. Park further away and walk a mile or two to save a few pounds.

463.   Stop viewing a few pounds as something that "doesn't matter." A few pounds spent repeatedly adds up to a lot of debt, and the reverse is also true: if you save a few pounds repeatedly, you will save a fortune.

464.   If you're becoming stressed about money, take the focus off your own concerns and offer to help someone else. Busying your mind is the best way to distract yourself from money worries. If you stop obsessing about them, they will sort themselves out.

465.   Have a toast party for your kids. Put all the toppings you can think of in the centre of the table and let them help themselves. They will think this is a real treat and it's a low-cost activity. Chocolate spread and marshmallows seem to go down particularly well!

466. Designate certain weekends "free" weekends and see what creative ideas you can come up with. Whenever you allow yourself no other option, it's amazing what you can think of.

467. Teach your kids the value of money with rewards for extra chores. Think of the money you spend in terms of how long it would take to earn it too. Is it worth an hour's work just to buy a candle? Or whatever you're considering buying? If it is worth it to you, that's fine. But determine if it's worth it to you instead of just mindlessly buying stuff.

468. Make a list of every film or boxset you want to watch and work your way through them. Make full use of whatever streaming service you have.

469. Don't get a TV license. There is plenty to watch that doesn't come from live TV. Just make sure you submit the form stating that you don't need a TV license because you won't be using iPlayer or live services and stick to it, so you don't get fined.

470. Only park your car in places you know you can't get a ticket. Be careful of time limits and make sure you keep a record of your arrival time.

471. Drive below the speed limit. Make sure you don't get unnecessary tickets and charges.

472. Buy a soap dispenser and fill it with half water, half hand soap so you aren't buying soap as often.

473. If you have an open fire, use it instead of the heating. Make your own firelighters with newspapers. You can google how to make them. You just fold them a bit like a fan.

474. Learn about how to go foraging. Read about all the safe fruits and vegetables and mushrooms you can find in the wild and eat.

475.   Use fresh mint or lemon balm to make tea. You can easily make an infusion by adding boiled water and it's cheaper than buying herbal tea if you already have it growing in your garden.

476.   If you go to fast food places, only buy food off the "savers" menu. If you're hungry, buy two cheap burgers rather than one large one that costs five times as much.

477.   Buy or make a refillable advent calendar. Add little notes to it with Christmas activities you can do together each day or buy nets of foil wrapped chocolates and fill the pockets with them.

478.   Don't compare yourself to others. It will make you buy things to try to keep up, but whatever you buy, it will never be enough.

479.   Come to an agreement with friends that you don't buy each other presents. Just make a kind gesture instead, bake them something or write them a thoughtful note. Our love doesn't have to be shown through our spending.

480.   Don't buy lots of food from health food stores unless you have specifically factored it into your budget. They usually charge triple the price of other supermarkets.

481.   Only boil the amount of water you actually need in the kettle. Don't waste energy heating water you won't use.

482.   If you have an immersion heater you use, set an alarm when you turn it on to remind you to turn it off again! (This tip definitely comes from personal experience!)

483.   If you are eating out with kids, find out where kids can eat free. You might have to dine out on a Wednesday, but the savings are worth it, and it will be less busy too.

484.   Use free trials to see what you think of new services but remember to cancel them right before the trial ends – unless it's something that adds a lot of value to your life.

485.   Order your food shopping online. You might have to pay a little extra to have it delivered, but it means you won't be tempted to look around or buy anything that wasn't on the list, and it saves you petrol and the time spent picking everything too.

486.   Don't always buy new clothes for your kids. I have found so many amazing bargains second hand for my kids. Look for clothing bundles on eBay and Vinted too. Kids get clothes stained and outgrow them so quickly that there is no point in spending a lot of money on their clothes.

487.   Before you make a purchase, ask yourself if you already own something that serves the same purpose, or that looks similar to it.

488.   Use a shopping basket instead of a trolley. Limit yourself to two bags of groceries. I always spent next to nothing on groceries whenever I didn't have a car and I could only buy what I could carry home.

489.   Get baby items second hand or ask family and friends if they have any they aren't using at the moment. You can always give them back whenever you're finished with them, and they can use them again.

490.   Look out for parades, community fun days and light switch on events. These are all free to attend and they always have a wonderful atmosphere.

491.   Look out for events organised through your kids' schools. They often offer quiz nights, group trips to pantomimes, seasonal markets, uniform fairs and barbecues.

492.   Look out for local youth clubs for your children to attend. They are cheap to attend, and they get to socialise with kids their age. Sign up for Brownies, Cubs and other church organised clubs like this. They are much more affordable than private classes and clubs.

493.   Don't buy very expensive toilet roll. You will get used to the cheaper stuff and not all of it is worse than the branded kind.

494.   Don't put yourself in your places of temptation. You know where these are better than anyone. They are unique to each of us.

495.   Give yourself affordable touches of luxury. Take a trip into town and treat yourself to a single bath product, a second-hand book or a cup of hot chocolate in a hotel. If you do it infrequently, you will value it all the more.

496.   Get a copy of Dining of a Dime cookbook and any books by Kate Singh relating to budgeting from Amazon. They are hugely inspiring.

497.   Look for tablecloths and curtains in charity shops. Cover your table to make it last longer. I didn't do this and ours is now covered in paint stains and dye! Get heavier curtains that adequately insulate your doors and windows.

498.   Heat the room you're using and keep the doors closed to contain the heat. Don't open the windows at the same time as having the heating on. (This might seem obvious, but it can be easy to overlook these things!)

499.   Get vegetables that are multifunctional. Buy a pumpkin, use the flesh for soup, roast the seeds and use the empty pumpkin as a bird feeder. Fill it with seeds and tie it up with string. Just make sure it is well supported. We didn't do this once and it fell and made a huge mess all over the garden! And remember that we all learn most from our mistakes, financial and otherwise!

500.   To finish off, I wanted to say don't be afraid to be frugal. Be proud of your frugality and your small savings. They will add up to huge ones over the course of years and completely change your financial future.

Printed in Great Britain
by Amazon

28645254R00040